GAUGUIN

GAUGUIN

TEXT BY

JOHN RUSSELL

A MENTOR-UNESCO ART BOOK

PUBLISHED BY
THE NEW AMERICAN LIBRARY, NEW YORK AND TORONTO
BY ARRANGEMENT WITH UNESCO

FIRST PRINTING, DECEMBER, 1968

MENTOR TRADEMARK REG. U. S. PAT. OFF. AND FOREIGN COUNTRIES
REGISTERED TRADEMARK — MARCA REGISTRADA

MENTOR-UNESCO ART BOOKS ARE PUBLISHED IN THE UNITED STATES BY
THE NEW AMERICAN LIBRARY, INC.,
1301 AVENUE OF THE AMERICAS, NEW YORK, NEW YORK 10019,
IN CANADA BY THE NEW AMERICAN LIBRARY OF CANADA LIMITED,
295 KING STREET EAST, TORONTO 2, ONTARIO
PRINTED IN ITALY BY AMILCARE PIZZI S.P.A. MILANO

Paul Gauguin was born in 1848, a year of great social upheaval. Upheaval predominated, equally, in the private history of his own family. But neither in European politics nor in the turbulent activity of his parents and grandparents was there a sequence of events more extraordinary, more genuinely and meaningfully dramatic, than that which marked Gauguin's career as a painter. What others have dreamed of doing, Gauguin actually did: he lived his ideas to the point at which they destroyed him. In so doing, he led a legendary life. But the legend relates more to the man than to the work: the really important thing about Gauguin is that he was perseverance personified.

Had he not been perseverance personified, he would not have been able to bring about, almost single-handed, the renewal of painting. In his art, as in his medical history, he would have gone down for ever, beyond recapture and beyond recall. What happened was precisely the contrary: even when he was dying, a man broken in body in his early fifties, he was painting as well as ever; and in his last notes on the nature of art he achieved, if anything, an ever greater lucidity and objectivity. He remained to the end the man who once said that although his own paintings were only relatively good he had at least struck a blow, and a lasting one, on behalf of the painters of our own century.

Gauguin's apprenticeship, insofar as he had one, is so unlike the apprenticeship of any other major painter that it is worthwhile to examine it in some detail. From infancy—from the day of his birth, almost, since there

5

was fighting in the streets of Paris when he was barely a week old—he lived with violence and the memory of violence. His maternal grandfather served a long prison sentence for attempting to murder his wife. (That same grandfather had previously been jailed for attempting to rape his own daughter, later to be Gauguin's mother.) When he was a year old his parents took him to Peru, where Madame Gauguin had rich relations: on the voyage out, conditions were such that Gauguin's father died of a heart attack while the ship was still at sea. Gauguin was left in no doubt therefore that life was a desperate affair. But he also inherited from his maternal grandmother a belief in the sovereign power of ideas. His grandmother, best known by her maiden name, Flora Tristan, was a nineteenth-century radical in the great tradition: a militant thinker for whom an idea was something to be thought through and acted upon at no matter what risk to oneself. One of the best of her books has a title which her grandson might well have adopted, had he wished to write his memoirs of life in the South Seas: *Peregrinations of a Pariah* (*Pérégrinations d'une Paria*, 1838).

So Gauguin very soon learned what life was about, in terms of other people's experience. As far as he himself was concerned his experience in boyhood was full of contradictions. Paradise, where Peru was in question, was both found and lost. Found, because his circumstances there were ideally agreeable: lost, because he was taken back to France after only four years. Gauguin had felt very much at home in Peru—his great-grandmother had claimed to be descended from Montezuma—and he lived there in an environment where money and power were taken for granted. A connection of his mother's was President of the Republic at the time, and although Gauguin never said so explicitly it was natural that he should associate happiness and fulfilment with far countries and exotic ways of life, just as it is inconceivable that France was not associated for him, from 1855 onwards, with misery and confinement and restriction. For someone who spoke only Spanish, to begin with, and was used to an altogether gentler and lazier and more privileged way of life, schooldays in France were purgatorial. Gauguin thought only of how to get away; eventually, in 1865, he did get away by apprenticing himself to go to sea on a three-masted ship. He stayed at sea more or less uninterruptedly for six years.

In this way Gauguin got through the years of adolescence and early manhood without running parallel at any point to the conventional " artist's education ". He disembarked at Toulon as a free man, in April 1871, with no idea at all of art—save, perhaps, for the Peruvian idols which he remembered clearly from his childhood. He was a difficult character—so much so that his mother feared that he would never come to terms with the ordinary workings of society—and he had always been quick, even with his superiors at sea, to resent any infringement of his freedom. But he had learned in the Navy that there is a right and a wrong way of doing things: method was all, on shipboard. When his guardian found him a post in a stockbroker's office in Paris he applied the same principle to his duties there; and before long he was doing unusually well.

Gauguin's mother had died in 1867; but his guardian, Gustave Arosa, was not a man to take his duties lightly. Not only did he find Gauguin a job, but he took him into his own home. In this way, Gauguin was given the run of one of the most rewarding private collections of the day: Arosa was an enthusiast for Courbet, Delacroix, Corot, Daumier and Jongkind, and in every case he had proved himself a fastidious judge. Gauguin took to painting himself, in an amateurish way, and he also took to going to the galleries. None of this came out very strongly—his wife said later that at the time of their marriage in 1873 she had no idea that Gauguin was interested in art—but by the mid-eighteen-seventies Gauguin's position in society was consolidated, and with prosperity there came an ever more evident dedication to art. His own painting began to be vindicated, however modestly, when he showed for the first time at the Salon in 1876. He also made his mark as a collector: between 1876 and 1880 he spent what was by the standards of the day a small fortune on impressionist paintings; even if he had never painted himself he would have a modest place in art history for his collection of paintings by Manet, Pissarro, Cézanne, Monet, Degas, Renoir, Sisley and Mary Cassatt.

By 1880 Gauguin was rich, settled, well-housed, well-mated, and the father of three children whom he adored. He was also getting more and more of a grip on the problems of painting. In 1879 he had even contributed a small statuette to the fourth Impressionist Exhibition on the Avenue de l'Opéra. In 1880, when the fifth show in the series came round, he was allowed to exhibit no fewer than seven paintings. J.-K. Huysmans may have marked them down as " watered-down Pissarro", but to be there at all was a remarkable achievement for a man of affairs who nine years before had hardly seen a paint-brush, let alone touched one. He owed it in part to the advocacy of Pissarro, who had been a friend of his since 1876; but neither for the quality of his work nor for his attitude to the other exhibitors could he be classed as a humble beginner. He was a tough-minded individual who could hold his own in debate; and when the pioneers of impressionism began to quarrel among themselves he was not the man to sit silent and listen. It was soon clear to him not merely that the impressionists were finished as a coherent group of friends, but that impressionism itself was finished as an instrument of original expression. There was nothing more to be done with it. It could still prompt a great masterpiece like Renoir's *Déjeuner des Canotiers* (1879); but as a working principle it had to give way to something else. Gauguin did not yet know what that " something else " would be, but he set himself to find out.

Impressionism had been before all things a school of truth to Nature: or truth, more exactly, to the impressions which Nature has to offer. It was a physical art, an art of immediate perception, an intuitive and all but mindless art. It was not the artist's rôle to adjust or modify or reorganise his sensations, but simply to set them down as directly and as truthfully as he could. It was also a completely impartial art. Private feelings played no part in it, even if the impact of a great impressionist painting

Paul Gauguin. (Collection Viollet.)

is now recognised as primarily euphoric. When Millet painted peasants in the field, and when Van Gogh painted his own boots, there was in each case an element of social protest; Monet also had his difficult days, but it did not occur to him to refer to the fact in his work. Any kind of enduring general comment upon the conditions of life would, in fact, have been contrary to the principles of impressionism, which is by definition an art of the fugitive moment.

Gauguin had quite another ambition. He believed that it was the duty of the artist to make use of Nature and not simply to bow down before her. As for the imitation of Nature, that was an even grosser error, and one which had bedevilled art since the days of Periclean Athens. There was something effete, something positively distasteful, about the passivity of the impressionists in the face of Nature. Even they themselves felt this: for, one after the other, they turned revisionist. Manet remembered his passion for Velasquez. Renoir in the eighteen-eighties turned to a classicizing, pre-ordained way of rendering the figure. Pissarro tinkered with divisionism. Monet alone remained true to the initial faith. The mid-eighteen-eighties were a time for re-thinking and regrouping, on almost every hand.

It was to devote himself uninterruptedly to this problem that Gauguin resigned, in January 1883, from the firm in which he had made such a comfortable living. Gauguin had an exalted view of the nature of art: he did not at all see the painter as a mere receiving station, attentive to the least flicker of the world around him and far too docile to impose upon his sensations an order of his own devising. On the contrary: *everything* was in painting. Literature, direct observation, a virtuosity that went far beyond mere everyday skill, a gift of individual vision, and even music—all of them were somehow a part of painting. At the same time, he did not believe in the idea of a completely original genius: the best that any painter could hope for was to add one link to the chain that others had begun.

So it was not from any wild expressionistic impulse that

Gauguin left the money-market. That market was in disorder throughout the year 1882, and Gauguin was one of many who had lost money instead of making it. There was a risk in going over completely to painting, but it was not quite so senseless a risk as some commentators have suggested. Nor were Gauguin's family difficulties altogether his fault. His Danish wife had never been schooled to the kind of life which a Monet or Pissarro took for granted in bad days; life in a rented house in Rouen was dismal enough, after the years of prosperity in Paris, but even worse was life in Copenhagen, with her family united against Gauguin and herself forced to eke out a living by giving lessons in French. Gauguin had no success when he tried to rebuild a life in business, and he had hardly more success with his paintings. Contrary to legend, Gauguin did not " give up everything " when he resigned from his position as a stockbroker. He genuinely tried to keep his family together, if not by the sale of his paintings, then by the renewed use of his business abilities. If, eventually, he gave up the attempt, the fault was as much theirs as his.

Meanwhile the bad winter of 1884-85 had at least the merit of precipitating Gauguin's ideas about painting. He was in Copenhagen at the time, and a crucial letter to his friend the painter Schuffenecker, dated 14 January 1885, has survived to show us exactly what was on his mind. Not many letters have been as fateful for the future of art: for Gauguin had thought his way through to the renewal of painting, and what he drew up for Schuffenecker's perusal was nothing less than the charter of the twentieth-century painter—a list, in other words, of the conditions within which he could go to work with some possibility of success.

He had decided, for instance, that a painting is before all things a portrait of the artist. It may be a still life, or a landscape, or a figure-subject. It may even be a portrait of someone else. None the less, in every case, the painter himself is portrayed. The artist was not merely a paragon of receptivity: he was a man who knew how to organise his perceptions in the way that best accorded with his

11

Rouen. The Blue Roofs. 1884. Canvas, 74 x 60 cm. Oskar Reinhart Collection, Winterthur (Switzerland).

own nature. He was intelligent in the highest possible degree, and what he had to communicate was something that could not be found in Nature, ready-made. Nor could it be put into words, or indeed formulated in any other way. It was himself, his own inmost being in the quintessence of its deepest responses to life.

It followed from this that the genuine artist gave the world a particular and an unmistakable look. His pictures, like his handwriting, revealed him completely. Graphologists could distinguish between a truthful and an untruthful handwriting; and anyone who loved painting and knew how to analyse it correctly could soon see exactly what kind of a man had painted a particular picture. Cézanne, for instance, was in Gauguin's view something of an Eastern mystic—" He has the face of a Levantine ancient " —and what he sought for in his forms was the ponderous tranquillity of a man who has stretched his length on the ground, the better to dream his dreams through to the end. His colour, again, had the gravity of the wise men of the East. As a man of the South, also, Cézanne would spend whole days reading Virgil on the top of a mountain and looking at the sky. Therefore, Gauguin concluded, " his horizons are lofty, his blues very intense, and his reds amazingly vibrant ".[1]

Gauguin insisted, in this same letter, on the way in which every part of the picture was permeated by the painter's individual personality. In a Raphael, *everything* said " Raphael ". In Carolus Duran, a landscape was as obscene as a nude. But, at the same time, there were certain fundamental and ever-valid principles which, once learned, would simplify the painter's task. Every colour had, for instance, its own specific emotional connotation. There were colours that stood for nobility, and others that stood for the vulgar and the commonplace. There were colours that stood for excitement, and others that stood for calm and consolation. If the sycamore stood for sadness, it was not because people associated it with cemeteries, but because the colour of its leaves was basically sad and could not be otherwise. Similarly with line: there were lines that stood for energy and aggression, and others that

13

stood for weakness and passivity. The so-called " weeping willow " had its name for a good reason: lines that bend over and downward have a depressive connotation. It is a fact of universal experience that a line which begins in the bottom left corner of a painting and moves diagonally upwards towards the right has a tonic effect upon us. Conversely, a line that moves diagonally upwards from the bottom right corner has in our eyes a defensive look. These are matters of universal instinct: no amount of " education " will prevail against them. It is the rôle of the artist to turn them to his own purposes. He can do this by virtue of his being more alert than other men, more aware of his own inner processes, and better able to organise them: more intelligent, in a word.

At the moment of writing, it would have seemed extravagant even to Gauguin's devoted friend " Schuff " if someone had said: "A great part of the art of the next century will derive from this letter." Gauguin was not, at this time, a prominent figure, and those who met him casually, or saw him from a distance, remarked on his bizarre and disquieting appearance. The painter Jacques-Émile Blanche saw him, for instance, at Dieppe in the summer of 1885; and he wrote many years later that Gauguin's haggard looks and eccentric way of dressing were among the symptoms which his father, the famous Dr. Blanche, had always regarded as signs of megalomania. If it is megalomania to see oneself as the saviour of painting, then there would be something in the diagnosis. But to most painters of our time, Gauguin's letter is both a charter of liberation and proof of a superior wisdom. It set out once and for all the principles upon which a new kind of painting could be based. Gauguin himself could not operate in this way for a number of years to come, but there were already others—Seurat, above all—who happened upon them at around the same time.

Gauguin was not at all the impulsive, improvisatory artist of legend. When he went down to Brittany in February 1888, he explained to his wife that although the season was unfavourable to his health he was a man who needed to work for six, seven or even eight months at a time in one and the same place. He needed to penetrate a landscape completely before he could master it. Good painting could only come from a complete knowledge of both a countryside and the people who inhabited it. It was, in any case, one thing to have the right idea and quite another to act it out to one's satisfaction. In 1902, when he was already mortally ill in the South Seas, Gauguin looked back on his career and made the notes which were published in 1951 as *Racontars de rapin*. In these he likened himself to the savage who would sit, hour by hour, in silence and stillness until suddenly, with a single bound, he had his prey by the throat. This was how Gauguin regarded the art of the future. He knew that it was in his power to make it possible, but he also knew that it would take time, and patience, and a continual watchfulness, to bring it into being. As for the critic, he cared nothing for his opinion. How could people judge the old masters from the outside, when the painter, with all his special gifts and all his lifelong preoccupation with the subject, was still so far from having plumbed their depths? The so-called " informed critic " was informed about the past in the way that a civil engineer is informed about drainage: beyond that ... Whereas the artist represented the finest part of the nation. He it was who created the future, brought great gifts to mankind, and gave life a new meaning.

A critic may serve merely, as Gauguin said, to reel off the names in the catalogue. But he is entitled to remark, even so, that Gauguin's famous letter to Schuffenecker started a trail which Seurat, and which Munch, and which Matisse, and which Kandinsky, and which many a painter of our own day has been happy to follow. Seurat in his Port-en-Bessin seascapes, and even more so in his paintings of the circus and the night-café, was preoccupied with lines whose every direction had an emotional significance. (He reached a point at which even the forked line of a pair of coat-tails thrown high in the air had a specific meaning.) Munch's every painting was a portrait of his own tormented nature; and his anti-naturalistic use of colour had precisely the connotations which Gauguin had in mind. (When people say of a friend who lost his temper that " he saw red " they are following, however crudely, in Gauguin's footsteps.) Matisse produced, in the still life of oranges which now belongs to Picasso, one of the greatest of all acts of homage to Gauguin the colourist; and at the end of his life, in the *papiers découpés*, he gave colour precisely the liberty which Gauguin had always craved for it. Kandinsky went one further than Gauguin when he claimed to find the whole gamut of human feeling in the colours of the Kremlin churches. The abstract painting of the last few years, with its emphasis on large flat areas of pure colour, is in essence a derivation from Gauguin, who knew that eventually, in some way still hidden from him, colour would assert itself as the dominant element in painting. He knew nothing, of course, of abstract painting as it has developed more recently; but he had no greater praise for one of his own works than to say that it was thoroughly and venturesomely abstract— set free, in other words, from the descriptive and approximative function which had so long bedevilled the artist. " The self-portrait I made for Van Gogh ", he wrote to Schuffenecker on 8 October 1888, " seems to me one of my best things. It's so abstract that it's incomprehensible. The drawing is quite special: a complete abstraction. The eyes, the mouth, the nose, are like flowers from a Persian carpet. They also personify the symbolic side. The colour is far from nature. Imagine to yourself something vaguely reminiscent of pottery being baked in the kiln! Such reds, and such violets! And the eyes blazing away like the flames that come shooting out from the furnace! The eyes—that's where a painter's thoughts struggle for their lives! "[2]

Gauguin saw that struggle quite realistically, as a campaign to be fought out in terms of a lifetime. He loved his children, for instance, and it was torture to him not to see them. But when his wife wanted him to break his sojourn in Brittany and go off to Denmark to see them he refused. " Since I left Denmark ", he wrote to her in February 1888, " I have had to muster every particle of my moral strength. To do this I have hardened my heart,

"Bonjour, Monsieur Gauguin" (II). 1889. Canvas, 113 x 92 cm.
Národní galerie, Prague. (Photo Giraudon.)

more and more. All that sensitive part of me is now anaesthetized, and it would be dangerous for me if I were to see the children and then have to leave them again. You must remember that I have a double nature: I am a very sensitive creature, but I am also a Red Indian. The sensitive creature has now disappeared, and the Red Indian is free to march forward, upright, with his feet firmly on the ground."[3]

It was not only against his family that Gauguin hardened his heart. His fellow-painters suffered, likewise, from his inflexible determination to have his way. Around the time that Gauguin turned down his wife's invitation, Félix Fénéon, the most gifted critic of his day, was writing in the *Revue Indépendante* about the new trends in painting. " It's passable, as far as the artist is concerned ", Gauguin wrote to Schuffenecker about the references to himself, " but rather odd about his character. It appears that all the others are little angels who have had to put up with my bad habits. Well, that's how people write history."[4] The basic difficulty and unbiddableness of Gauguin's nature came out strongly in his relations with Van Gogh, as everyone knows. Writing to Émile Bernard from Arles, in December 1888, Gauguin put his strong forefinger on the root of the trouble: " Vincent and I don't agree at all about painting. He admires Daumier, Daubigny, Ziem and Rousseau the Great—all people I can't abide. And, on the contrary, he loathes Ingres, Raphael and Degas, three painters whom I admire. I end up by saying 'Of course you're right, old man', for the sake of peace. He likes what I do: but when I produce a picture he always finds fault with it. He's a romantic. I'm much more drawn to a primitive way of thinking and acting..."[5]

This is an important letter in more ways than one. It stresses the classicising, monumental side of Gauguin's ambition, and it also stresses his longing to cut back through the Renaissance, through the Hellenistic tradition, to an earlier and more primitive mode of vision. The legend of Gauguin in the South Seas is that of an outcast who worked in an isolation that was as much moral as physical and had altogether turned his back on Europe.

18

In point of fact, however, he was in touch with Paris till the very end; and if he had not been a man of profound culture and wide sensibility it is unthinkable that a man like Stéphane Mallarmé would have agreed to act as chairman at the dinner which was held in Gauguin's honour on the eve of his departure for the South Seas. He knew from the first that his nature was a difficult one, and that it would be easier for him to have success of a kind if he suppressed certain areas of it. It dismayed him not at all that his friends talked, for instance, of his mysticism as if it were some strange complaint that would be better got rid of. " One must follow one's own temperament ", he wrote to Schuffenecker on 16 October 1888, " I know quite well that I shall be understood *less and less*. What does it matter if I draw away from the others? For the masses I shall be a riddle, for one or two people I shall be a poet, and sooner or later whatever is good about me will get to be acknowledged." " Never mind! ", he went on, " No matter what happens, I can tell you one thing: I shall end up by doing *first-class work*. I'm convinced of it. Just let's wait and see. You know as well as I do that where art is concerned I'm always right in the end."[6]

Throughout the late eighteen-eighties, Gauguin went at his task bull-headed: or, as he himself said, like an express train. He saw himself as an engine-driver: looking out of his cabin, he could see his destination far ahead and he knew that he was on the right track. But equally, as he also said, he was quite likely to go off the rails... All else was sacrificed to the struggle. " Schuff " was once again his confident when, on 13 November 1888, he outlined his way of life. " Good health, independence in one's work, and regular love-making—that's the secret. I can see your eyes open wide, dear virtuous Schuff, at these venturesome words! But don't get excited—eat properly, make love properly, work properly, and you'll die happy."[7]

These are not at all the accents of the weak-minded and self-indulgent beachcomber who staggers in and out of many a fictional account of Gauguin's career. He gave in to his body, in the end, but he never gave in to the mental frailties, the diminished grasp of reality, which are the marks, even to-day, of so many an exiled painter. Nor did he attempt the short cut to fulfilment which is another of the temptations of exile. He always had in mind the example of his heroes, most of whom had adjusted the language of the past, as he was trying to do, to the language of the future. Ingres, for instance, had had one eye on the antique and another on Nature: the creation, in this way, of a noble and logical pictorial language seemed to Gauguin one of the glories of nineteenth-century France, and an achievement which amply made up for the loss of Alsace and Lorraine. What were military setbacks in comparison with pictures that conquered the whole of Europe and ensured the freedom of painting for a generation and more?

He knew that art was an immensely difficult and complex business: and one in which the painter himself, as much as his work, is on trial. When he was in Brittany he pinned up on the walls of his room a print by Utamaro and reproductions of paintings by Fra Angelico, Botticelli, Manet (*Olympia*) and Puvis de Chavannes; he revered Degas, not only as a great painter, but as a man who personified the dignity of art; he remembered the overwhelming power of the Peruvian idols which he had seen as a child, and the hieratic, anti-naturalistic presence of the Egyptian and Assyrian and Far Eastern sculptures which he had seen in the Louvre; from Brittany he remembered, as much as anything, certain Romanesque carvings near Pont-Aven. In many of these things he was far ahead of his time: it was not, for instance, till some years after Gauguin's death in 1903 that Matisse and Derain and Picasso tried to annex for painting the magic force which emanates from African and Oceanic art.

The point of Gauguin is that he never drew back from any part of his nature or any one of his preoccupations. In this context he never forgot what Brunetière, then the great literary critic of the day, had said to Puvis de Chavannes: " I must congratulate you on having painted great pictures that are always subdued in tone. Never once have you used gaudy colours ..." Gauguin loved Puvis, but he knew that his own imperious nature would never make do with subdued colours or shudder at the notion of gaudy ones. If he went to the South Seas it was not to evade life but to get more deeply and more meaningfully into it: after the *Exposition Universelle* of 1889, where the Far Eastern pavilions had a profound effect upon him, he saw the East as the place of all places in which every side of his nature would be reconciled. As he wrote to Émile Bernard in June 1890: " A great thought-system is written in letters of gold in Far Eastern art, and I think that I could renew myself out there. The Occident at this moment has gone to rot, and a strong man could redouble his strength, like Antaeus, simply by setting foot in the Far East. A year or two later one could come back, a new man."[8]

That was not how it worked out for Gauguin himself. The relationship between himself, Europe, and the South Seas turned out to be a great deal more complex. The South Seas set him free from Europe, in an obvious pictorial sense, and they also provided him with a ready-made structure of dreams and superstitions and strange fealties which he could take over when he felt like it. He was able in this way to pose questions indirectly, and to give a slanting view of European predicaments, where he might not have cared to tackle the subjects head-on—or would, perhaps, have tackled them awkwardly and unsuccessfully. But he was very far from getting from the South Seas a simple chromatic charge of the kind which Nolde, or which Matisse, got from their briefer visits to Oceania. The charm of his South Seas pictures, for the casual visitor to museums, lies in the perfect authenticity of their picturesque detail: but for those who prize Gauguin above all for his rôle in the renewal of painting it lies rather in the insistence with which Gauguin returns to European models: to the recumbent Venus of Giorgione, for instance, in the *Queen of Beauty* of 1896, now in the Pushkin Museum in Moscow, and to the earthly paradise of Puvis de Chavannes in more than one of the many-figured frieze-paintings of his last years. It was not by accident that when Gauguin died the painting on his easel was a view of a Breton village in the snow, or that during his last illness he pressed upon a visitor his copy of Mallarmé's *L'Après-Midi d'un faune*, illustrated by Manet. Gauguin was concerned to the end with European art, and with the ways in which it could be carried forward. The experience of the South Seas allowed him, as it were, to cut away the fat of European life; but it also enabled him to work in isolation from the "artists' life" of his native country. He had spoken of one of his Breton pictures as being " not at all Degas-like ... Japanese, rather, and painted by a savage from Peru ". But when he was actually cut off from Europe, and was free to paint subjects which were un-European in the highest possible degree, he harked back again and again to the break-through which he had made in France. It is because he made that break-through, and not because he led a " romantic " life in the South Seas, that so many of his successors owe him a great debt.

We can decipher that debt when we look at early paintings by Bonnard and Vuillard, with their arbitrary flat patterning and disdain for conventional perspective. Here it is the picture-language, not the feeling behind it, which was invaluable. The last thing that Bonnard and Vuillard wanted was to paint like Peruvian savages, but they were quick to see what they could take from Gauguin's example. We decipher the debt, equally, in Matisse's case. Matisse bought a small head of a boy by Gauguin early on in his career; and when he came to paint the great *Joie de vivre* which is now in the Barnes collection there was in it a good deal of the Gauguin who tried, over and over again, to revive the great tradition of European pastoral. The famous portrait of Madame Matisse (autumn, 1905) with a vertical green stripe down the middle of her face would, again, have been unthinkable without the pungency and forthrightness of Gauguin's example. Gauguin's flat tones and radical contouring were fundamental to Matisse's procedures at that time, just as the great paintings now to be seen in Moscow and Leningrad owed much to Gauguin's readiness to let flat, unaccented colour-areas overwhelm the spectator.

Gauguin was, again, a man for whom untruth and

venality were crimes against the human spirit. People, he knew, were more likely to sell than to give themselves; and he saw his painting as part of a holy war against this state of affairs. Not that he had anything against selling his pictures: he kept to the end the instincts of a successful business man. What he objected to was a stingy, anal, ungiving attitude in human relations. In this, he was at one with the painters of the *Brücke* in Dresden. E.L. Kirchner and his colleagues were up against a society even more repulsive, and more hostile to art, than the Paris and the Copenhagen which rejected Gauguin. In using colour to express emotional truth, as distinct from conventional " accuracy ", the *Brücke* group followed on directly from Gauguin's example. They saw that example in terms of the freedom of the individual spirit, and not at all as a mere experiment in style. Gauguin, for them, had reasserted the dignity of man.

Munch, likewise, was out to make the truth known. That truth, in his view, was predominantly tragic in its implications, and he saw no reason why art should conceal it. His visions of disease, death, betrayal and pointless grief called for the colours of cruelty, and he proved himself able to reinvent those colours over and over again. Very different, but no less directly related to Gauguin, was the consistent euphoria of *fauve* painting as practised by Derain, by Dufy, by van Dongen and by Manguin and others. There is nothing in these paintings to call for a change in society, but there is a great deal that calls for a change in painting: and Gauguin is the grandfather of that change. Wherever painting has progressed beyond a commonplace naturalism, Gauguin has had something to do with it.

Above all, he encouraged his successors to push their ideas to the limit. " I have tried ", he said towards the end, " to vindicate the right to dare anything." Every word in this sentence counts: there was " the right ", to begin with, and there was the element of fearlessness. The two in combination led Gauguin into strange places, in life, and they led him to paint pictures which even to-day have not yielded up all their secrets. But if every subsequent generation of painters has addressed him with a heartfelt " Thank you " it is as much for his moral as for his technical example. Once again, his letters are the key to his nature. In October 1888 he wrote to Émile Bernard's sister in terms which can be transposed for the use of everyone, man or woman, painter or stockbroker or garage-hand, who wants to be a complete human being.

" If you want to go through life like the majority of young girls, pointlessly and with no one goal in mind, a prey to all the hazards which wealth brings as surely as poverty, dependent upon a society which takes so much and gives so little in return—if that is your ambition, don't bother to read on. But if you want to be *someone*, and to derive your sole and entire happiness from your own independent nature and your free conscience, then . . . you must know that you have a duty towards your fellow-beings. That duty is based upon loving-kindness, and upon sacrifice at all times. Let your conscience be your only judge. You must raise an altar to your dignity and your intelligence, and to nothing else. . . Be proud, but make sure that you have the right to be proud: but abolish all vanity. Vanity is for the mediocre... "9

It was because he had these principles, and lived them through, that Gauguin was able to renew the art of painting, and to make it possible for others to do the same.

ILLUSTRATIONS

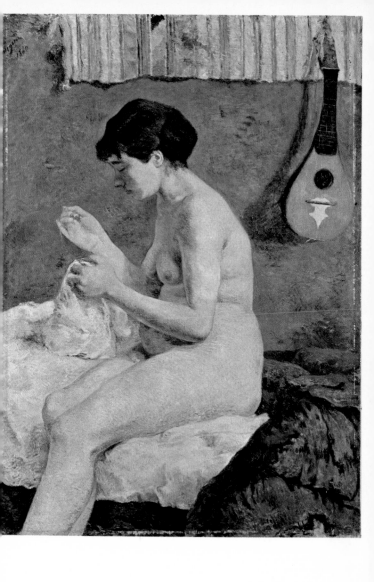

1

2

4

5

6

9

Vahine no te Tiare

P. Gauguin 91

14

IA ORANA MARIA

17

Gauguin 93.   Tehura

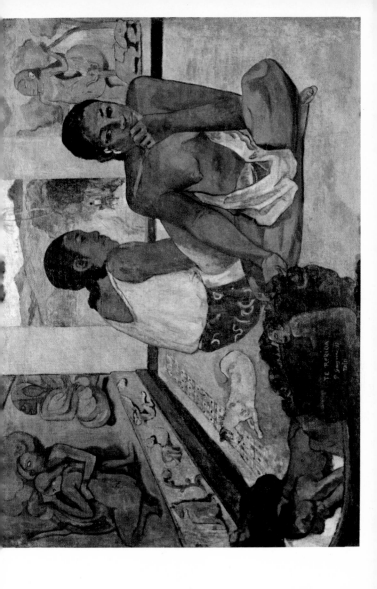

23

CONTENTS

CONTENTS

BIBLIOGRAPHY

COOPER, Douglas, *Gauguin*, Catalogue of exhibition at the Tate Gallery London, 1955.

DANIELSSON, Bengt, *Gauguin in the South Seas*, translated by Reginald Spink, London, Allen and Unwin, 1965.

GAUGUIN, Paul, *Avant et après*, Paris, G. Crès & Cie, 1923.

GAUGUIN, Paul, *Lettres à sa femme et à ses amis*, Paris, Bernard Grasset, 1949.

GAUGUIN, Paul, *Lettres à Daniel de Monfreid*, Paris, Falaize, 1950.

GAUGUIN, Paul, *Racontars de rapin*, Paris, Falaize, 1951.

GOLDWATER, Robert, *Paul Gauguin*, Paris, Nouvelles Editions françaises, 1957.

PERRUCHOT, Henri, *Gauguin*, translated by Humphrey Hare, London, Perpetua Books, 1963; Cleveland, World Publishing Co., 1964.

REWALD, John, *Post-Impressionism: from Van Gogh to Gauguin*, New York, Museum of Modern Art, 1956.

SUTTON, Denys; PICKVANCE, Ronald, *Gauguin and the Pont-Aven Group*, Catalogue of exhibition at the Tate Gallery, London, 1966.

WILDENSTEIN, Georges, *Gauguin*, Vol. 1, Catalogue, Paris, Les Beaux-Arts, 1964.

NOTES

1. Translated from Paul GAUGUIN, *Lettres à sa femme et à ses amis*, Paris, Bernard Grasset, 1949, pp. 45-46.

2. ID., pp. 140-141.

3. ID., p. 126.

4. ID., p. 128.

5. ID., p. 154.

6. ID., p. 147.

7. ID., p. 149.

8. ID., p. 193.

9. ID., pp. 137-138.

Printed in Italy